W9-COM-602

ALEXANDRIA OCASIO-CORTEZ

by Emma Kaiser

FOCUS READERS.

VOYAGER

www.focusreaders.com

Focus Readers is distributed by North Star Editions:
sales@northstareditions.com | 888-417-0195

Produced for Focus Readers by Red Line Editorial.

Content Consultant: Christina Bejarano, Professor of Multicultural Women's and Gender Studies, Texas Woman's University

Photographs ©: Michael Brochstein/Sipa USA/AP Images, cover, 1; lev radin/Shutterstock Images, 4–5, 45; Red Line Editorial, 7, 35; TierneyMJ/Shutterstock Images, 8–9; Elijah Lovkoff/Shutterstock Images, 11; Ron Edmonds/AP Images, 13; Matthew Kiernan/Alamy, 14–15; Gino Santa Maria/Shutterstock Images, 17; Terray Sylvester/VWPics/AP Images, 19; Katerine Welles/Shutterstock Images, 21; Evan Vucci/AP Images, 22–23; Nic Neufeld/Shutterstock Images, 25; Richard B. Leivine/Alamy, 26; Susan Walsh/AP Images, 28–29; Saul Loeb/AFP/Getty Images, 31; Josh Bachman/Zuma Press/Newscom, 33; MCL Yingling, 36–37; Alex Edelman/CNP/picture-alliance/dpa/AP Images, 39; Rachael Warriner/Shutterstock Images, 40, 42–43

Library of Congress Cataloging-in-Publication Data
Names: Kaiser, Emma, 1996- author.
Title: Alexandria Ocasio-Cortez / by Emma Kaiser .
Description: Lake Elmo, MN : Focus Readers, [2020] | Series: Groundbreaking
  women in politics | Includes bibliographical references and index. |
  Audience: Grades 4-6
Identifiers: LCCN 2019025937 (print) | LCCN 2019025938 (ebook) | ISBN
  9781644930892 (hardcover) | ISBN 9781644931684 (paperback) | ISBN
  9781644933268 (pdf) | ISBN 9781644932476 (ebook)
Subjects: LCSH: Ocasio-Cortez, Alexandria, 1989---Juvenile literature. |
  Women legislators--United States--Biography--Juvenile literature. |
  Legislators--United States--Biography--Juvenile literature. | United
  States. Congress. House--Biography--Juvenile literature.
Classification: LCC E901.1.O27 L35 2020 (print) | LCC E901.1.O27 (ebook)
  | DDC 328.73/092 [B]--dc23
LC record available at https://lccn.loc.gov/2019025937
LC ebook record available at https://lccn.loc.gov/2019025938

Printed in the United States of America
Mankato, MN
012020

ABOUT THE AUTHOR

Emma Kaiser has a bachelor's degree in English from the University of Northwestern, St. Paul and has worked in publishing for several years. She currently works as a writer and editor and lives with her husband in St. Paul, Minnesota.

TABLE OF CONTENTS

CHAPTER 1

AN UNEXPECTED VICTORY

In June 2018, Alexandria Ocasio-Cortez waited for the results of a Democratic **primary** election. A crowd of her supporters waited with her. The 28-year-old was running to be a Democratic nominee for the US House of Representatives. She hoped to represent New York's 14th **District**. This district included parts of Queens and the Bronx. Ocasio-Cortez had lived in the district for much of her life.

Before the 2018 race for New York's 14th District, Ocasio-Cortez had never run for office.

However, she was facing Joe Crowley. This powerful Democrat had served in the House of Representatives for 20 years. He had not faced a primary opponent in 14 years. Most experts thought Ocasio-Cortez had no chance against Crowley. She had much less experience and campaign money than he did.

But Ocasio-Cortez thought she could represent the 14th District better than Crowley could. That district was one of the most diverse areas of New York City. It was also a very low-income district. Ocasio-Cortez was of Puerto Rican descent. She knew what it was like to work for little pay. She shared struggles with many in her district.

The primary results came in on TV. Against all odds, Ocasio-Cortez had won the election. News reporters called it one of the biggest upsets of the 2018 elections.

With the win, Ocasio-Cortez became
the Democratic candidate for New York's
14th District. The district was heavily Democratic.
That made Ocasio-Cortez the clear favorite to win
the general election in November.

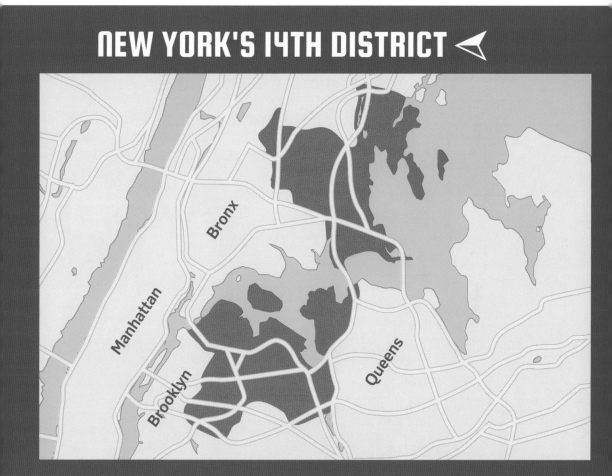

NEW YORK'S 14TH DISTRICT

CHAPTER 2

EARLY LIFE

Alexandria Ocasio-Cortez was born on October 13, 1989. She was born in the Parkchester neighborhood of the Bronx, New York. Alexandria's father, Sergio, was also born in the Bronx. Sergio was from a Puerto Rican family. He owned a small architecture company. Alexandria's mother, Blanca, was born in Puerto Rico. She earned a living by cleaning houses. Alexandria grew up speaking Spanish and English.

Approximately 1.5 million people live in the Bronx, New York.

She lived in the Bronx until she was five years old. Then, her family moved an hour north to Yorktown. This town is in Westchester County, a wealthy suburban area. Alexandria's parents wanted her and her younger brother to attend better schools. From an early age, Alexandria learned how much a neighborhood could affect a person's opportunities.

Alexandria was a good student. At Yorktown High School, she competed in an international science fair. She won second place in the microbiology category. Ocasio-Cortez finished high school in 2007. Then she attended Boston University. She studied economics and international relations.

During her second year at college, her father learned that he had lung cancer. He died at the age of 48. Her father had been the family's main

Boston University is one of more than 30 different colleges in the Boston area.

source of income. As a result, Ocasio-Cortez had to work two jobs to help her family make house payments. She worked these jobs while attending college full-time.

These experiences brought Ocasio-Cortez closer to **public policy** in more personal ways. She wasn't just studying the effects of expensive housing, low-paying jobs, and debt. She was experiencing them as a reality.

Ocasio-Cortez also gained political experience in college. She worked for Senator Edward Kennedy. In this position, Ocasio-Cortez helped with **immigration** cases. She was the only Spanish speaker on her team. And some **constituents'** sole language was Spanish. Ocasio-Cortez was the only one who could talk to those people.

Many of these constituents were trying to navigate the US immigration system. Others were trying to find family members who had been taken by Immigration and Customs Enforcement (ICE). This government agency is in charge of policing immigration laws. ICE also guards the country's borders.

On Kennedy's staff, Ocasio-Cortez learned about establishment politics as well. This type of politics refers to a system where certain people and groups hold large amounts of power.

Edward Kennedy was a US Senator for 47 years.

Ocasio-Cortez found that she disagreed with this kind of politics. She believed average people should have as much sway as those with wealth and connections.

Ocasio-Cortez became driven to help the people she felt the government had ignored. This purpose fueled her work and life, even before her career in politics.

CHAPTER 3

A CAREER IN POLITICS

In 2011, Alexandria Ocasio-Cortez graduated with honors from Boston University. After college, she returned to the Bronx. She went back to the neighborhood where she had grown up. She worked on supporting education in her Bronx community. For example, Ocasio-Cortez worked as an educational director at the National Hispanic Institute. In this position, she helped high school students build leadership skills.

Most Parkchester buildings are part of one large complex, which first opened in the 1940s.

Ocasio-Cortez also cared about helping children learn to read. So she started a company called Brook Avenue Press. The company made children's books with stories that took place in the Bronx. She wanted children to have books that showed the Bronx in a positive light.

However, Ocasio-Cortez also had to help her mother make ends meet. She took jobs waitressing and bartending. As a waitress, Ocasio-Cortez spoke to people from diverse backgrounds. She learned what people in the community cared about. She also developed tough skin. She learned to not take insults or criticism too personally.

Ocasio-Cortez returned to politics during the 2016 presidential campaign. She supported Bernie Sanders. He was much more **progressive** than the other candidates. During the campaign,

 Bernie Sanders gives a speech during his presidential campaign in 2016.

Ocasio-Cortez became more interested in political issues around the country. And she wanted to see places of political conflict in person. She decided to take a road trip.

First, Ocasio-Cortez drove from New York to Flint, Michigan. There, she talked with people affected by the Flint water crisis. Dangerous levels of lead had gotten into the city's water supply.

As a result, thousands of people had become ill. Ocasio-Cortez saw how government neglect had led to the problem. She also saw how people in Flint had suffered because of the crisis.

Next, Ocasio-Cortez traveled to North Dakota. She joined thousands of other protesters who opposed the construction of an oil pipeline on Sioux land. These protesters believed the pipeline was a threat to the area's clean water. They also believed the pipeline was a danger to ancient Sioux burial grounds. Ocasio-Cortez was inspired by the difference the protesters were making. She wanted to do more to help people. She realized

➤ THINK ABOUT IT

Why do you think the act of protesting made such an impact on Ocasio-Cortez? Have you ever spoken out against something you thought was wrong?

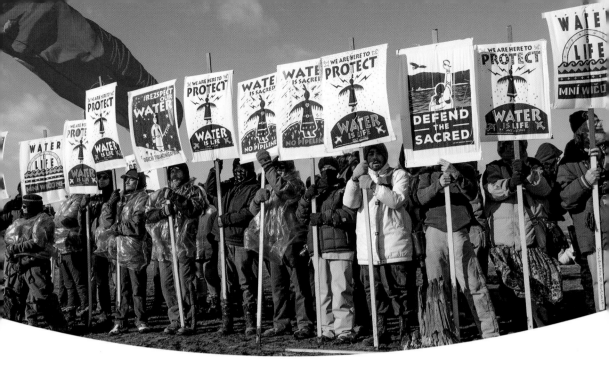

 Protesters hold signs to oppose an oil pipeline project on Sioux land.

that working in politics could be a good way to make positive change.

After Ocasio-Cortez returned home, she received a call from an organization known as Brand New Congress. The group was looking for new, progressive, working-class leaders. Brand New Congress wanted these leaders to run in the 2018 election. The group asked Ocasio-Cortez if she would run for Congress. She said yes.

BRAND NEW CONGRESS

Brand New Congress is a political group that backs candidates for Congress. The organization is run by former staffers from Bernie Sanders's 2016 presidential campaign. When Sanders lost the Democratic primary, his staffers began thinking about who should run for Congress. They wanted more progressive candidates.

Brand New Congress recruits nontraditional candidates. These candidates are suggested by everyday people. The candidates do not have to be members of a specific political party. Their views just have to be similar to Sanders's views. For example, Brand New Congress supports universal health care. Under this system, the government would provide medical care to all citizens, including people who cannot pay for the care.

Cori Bush was the first person backed by Brand New Congress. She ran unsuccessfully for the Missouri House.

Brand New Congress first looked for candidates for the 2018 elections. The group wanted diverse, working-class community leaders. Brand New Congress also wanted people who did not rely on powerful connections. The group received more than 11,000 names. One suggestion came from Alexandria Ocasio-Cortez's little brother, Gabriel. He believed his big sister would make a good candidate. She was exactly the kind of person Brand New Congress was looking for.

CHAPTER 4

THE PATH TO DC

Two main political parties exist in the United States. These parties are the Democratic Party and the Republican Party. Democrats tend to support greater social freedoms. They also believe the government should play an active role in the US economy. In contrast, Republicans tend to believe in keeping traditional social values. They also believe the government should not play an active role in the US economy.

In 2016, Democrat Hillary Clinton (right) ran against Republican Donald Trump for president.

Alexandria Ocasio-Cortez ran for Congress as a member of the Democratic Party. However, she was also a member of the Democratic Socialists of America (DSA). DSA is not a political party. But it is the largest **socialist** organization in the United States. Like other socialist groups, DSA does not support **capitalism**. Instead, the group believes the government should run most businesses and services. That way, the government could provide for people's basic needs, including housing, food, and health care.

Many Americans thought DSA's ideas were too extreme. However, the group's ideas were popular where Ocasio-Cortez was running for Congress. Voters in New York's 14th District were mostly low income. Ocasio-Cortez ran her campaign on issues that would improve those voters' lives. For example, she supported universal health care.

Members of the Democratic Socialists of America march during a parade in 2018.

She supported a higher minimum wage. And she supported free college education for all.

DSA backed Ocasio-Cortez's campaign. But she had a hard race ahead of her. Democrat Joe Crowley was a tough primary opponent. Voters already knew who he was. He also had the money of establishment politics on his side. With that money, Crowley could advertise a great deal on TV and other media.

⬛ Ocasio-Cortez's campaign posters included Spanish exclamation marks around her name.

To beat Crowley, Ocasio-Cortez needed to campaign in a different way. She developed a grassroots campaign. This type of campaign does not rely on much money. Instead, it depends on a large number of volunteers.

During the campaign, Ocasio-Cortez's volunteers made 170,000 phone calls to possible voters. Volunteers sent 120,000 text messages. They knocked on 120,000 doors as well.

Volunteers also created posters in both English and Spanish. Crowley's ads were only in English.

For his campaign, Crowley took big donations from large companies. Ocasio-Cortez relied on small donations from people. She spent much less than Crowley. Even so, the race was not close. Ocasio-Cortez won the primary with 57 percent of the votes. Crowley received only 43 percent.

After the primary, the hard part was over. Because the 14th District was very Democratic, Ocasio-Cortez easily beat the Republican candidate, Anthony Pappas. She received 78 percent of the votes. She was headed to Congress.

THINK ABOUT IT ◁

Why do you think Ocasio-Cortez's campaigning methods worked so well? In what ways did she connect with voters? What could Crowley have done differently?

CHAPTER 5

REPRESENTATIVE OCASIO-CORTEZ

On January 3, 2019, Alexandria Ocasio-Cortez was sworn in to the House of Representatives. She was 29 years old when she took office. That made her the youngest woman ever elected to Congress. But Ocasio-Cortez was not the only Democrat celebrating a big win. Democrats had won the majority in the House of Representatives. As a result, Democrats now controlled that chamber of Congress.

Ocasio-Cortez was sworn in to Congress with her mother (center) and House Speaker Nancy Pelosi.

Ocasio-Cortez helped form the most racially diverse Congress in US history. In the 2018 election, voters sent 24 new people of color to Congress. Voters also elected 42 new women. As a result, the House of Representatives included 102 women out of 435 total members. There were also 23 women in the Senate out of 100 total members. Women still made up less than 25 percent of Congress. But this Congress had more women than ever before.

After arriving in Congress, Ocasio-Cortez joined the House Oversight Committee. This committee oversees the US government. Its role includes looking into any presidential misconduct. Ocasio-Cortez also joined the House Financial Services Committee. This group oversees large banks. It also oversees how the government uses money on a national level.

▲ On January 4, 2019, all the female Democratic House members posed for a picture together.

While in Congress, Ocasio-Cortez wanted to work on many issues, such as for-profit prisons. The government runs most prisons. But for-profit prisons are run by private owners. Some people think these prisons often have worse conditions for inmates. Ocasio-Cortez did not think for-profit prisons should exist.

She also wanted to tackle problems with college student loans. The cost of attending US colleges had been rising for many years.

As a result, students have needed more and more loans to pay for college. Ocasio-Cortez wanted to find ways to lower this student debt.

Ocasio-Cortez wasted no time in getting to work. She joined a protest on her first day in Congress. The protesters gathered outside the office of House Speaker Nancy Pelosi. They wanted Pelosi to take action to address climate change.

Ocasio-Cortez also spoke out about immigration reform. Earlier that year, she had protested outside detention centers in Texas. President Trump had been separating undocumented immigrants from their children. Ocasio-Cortez opposed this policy. She believed it was cruel and wrong. In addition, she wanted to get rid of ICE. And she believed immigrants should have a clearer way to become US citizens.

▲ Ocasio-Cortez protests President Trump's immigration policy outside a detention center in Texas.

Ocasio-Cortez quickly gained huge amounts of attention. Some people loved and supported her. Others thought her ideas were too extreme or even un-American. She had barely arrived in Washington, DC. But she was already becoming one of the most talked-about names in politics.

SOCIAL MEDIA

Soon after Alexandria Ocasio-Cortez was elected, her fame rose. She was especially popular on social media platforms. Before she won the primary, she had 446,000 Twitter followers. Just months after she took office, she had more than 4.5 million followers.

In February 2019, a progressive website posted a video of Ocasio-Cortez to Twitter. She was talking about government corruption. The video was viewed more than 40 million times. Democrats realized Ocasio-Cortez's social media skill. They asked her to teach other members of Congress how to talk to constituents on Twitter.

Not all of the attention Ocasio-Cortez received was positive, however. She was a common target for conservative news outlets. Some tried to embarrass her. For instance, a Twitter user posted a video of her dancing in college. In response,

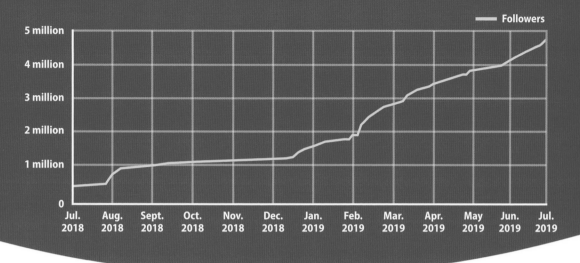

OCASIO-CORTEZ'S TWITTER FOLLOWERS

Ocasio-Cortez posted her own video. It showed her dancing into her new congressional office.

Ocasio-Cortez also used social media to relate to the public. On Twitter, she often asked for advice on everyday topics, such as planting a garden. On Instagram, she made live videos of herself doing regular tasks, such as cooking. During those livestreams, anyone online could ask her questions. People asked about policy, Congress, and her life in Washington, DC. Ocasio-Cortez used social media to make politics accessible, especially for young people.

CHAPTER 6

THE GREEN NEW DEAL

In 2018, the United Nations released two reports about climate change and **global warming**. These reports argued that **greenhouse gas emissions** needed to be cut in half by 2030. These emissions needed to be cut completely by 2050. Otherwise, many dangerous effects of global warming would become permanent.

Global warming is already melting Earth's ice caps. As a result, ocean levels are rising.

An ice cap in Greenland melts into the ocean.

Rising ocean levels threaten to flood many cities on the coasts. If the world's nations fail to stop global warming, people are likely to face more enormous problems. Climate change could increase the intensity of natural disasters. Climate change could also cause dirtier air and water. Many animal species could die out. Food supplies could run low. These effects could cost the United States many lives and trillions of dollars.

Alexandria Ocasio-Cortez believed the United States needed to act soon. In February 2019, she proposed her first piece of legislation. The legislation was called the Green New Deal. It was a 10-year plan. It called for the United States to stop using fossil fuels, including oil and coal. Using fossil fuels puts carbon into the atmosphere. This carbon contributes to climate change. The Green New Deal proposed to replace

⚑ On February 7, 2019, Ocasio-Cortez announced her Green New Deal legislation.

fossil fuels with renewable energy sources. These sources include wind and solar power.

The Green New Deal was inspired by the New Deal of the 1930s. The New Deal responded to the crisis of the Great Depression. Similarly, the Green New Deal was a response to the climate crisis. The plan also listed other goals. For example, it proposed a guarantee that every citizen would have a home, a job, and health care.

▲ Young activists protest in a senator's office to support the Green New Deal.

When the Green New Deal was announced, reactions were mixed. No Republicans supported the Green New Deal. Some Democrats did not support it either. Many critics thought the United States could not completely stop using fossil fuels. Many also thought it would be impossible to stop in only 10 years. After all, the United States was relying on fossil fuels for 80 percent of its energy.

However, many powerful members of Congress supported the Green New Deal. Some of them included 2020 presidential candidates such as Senator Kamala Harris, Senator Amy Klobuchar, and Senator Bernie Sanders. The public's concern for climate change had never been higher. Young people especially were demanding action.

In March 2019, the Senate voted on the Green New Deal. The bill did not receive enough votes to move forward. Even so, this defeat did not stop Ocasio-Cortez from speaking out about climate change. She continued to urge Congress to take action before it was too late.

THINK ABOUT IT ◁

The vast majority of scientists believe action is needed to address climate change. How can you tell your government to take action?

CHAPTER 7

LOOKING AHEAD

Alexandria Ocasio-Cortez became known as the face of the US progressive movement. In 2019, she appeared in a movie called *Knock Down the House*. The movie followed her 2018 congressional campaign. It followed other campaigns as well. The movie won awards at a film festival. It appeared on Netflix, too.

Knock Down the House showed viewers a closer look at Ocasio-Cortez's start in politics.

In May 2019, Ocasio-Cortez gave a speech about the need for a Green New Deal.

The movie allowed people to see inside her grassroots campaign. It portrayed Ocasio-Cortez in a positive way. She appeared invested in her community. She also appeared to be standing up for the underdog. People believed in her partly because she was also an underdog.

Ocasio-Cortez's story appealed to people as much as her politics did. Through her use of modern media, she got people's attention. She even reached individuals who normally paid little attention to politics. She made politics feel accessible to a larger number of voters. She also showed young people how they could have a role in their own government.

National news outlets called Ocasio-Cortez the future of the Democratic Party. However, many said she was also taking the party back to its roots. She reminded people of historic

▲ Voter turnout among young people was 10 percent greater in the 2018 election than in 2014.

Democratic figures. These Democrats worked for the people. They did not work just to gain power for themselves.

Ocasio-Cortez showed she was different from other politicians. People saw this difference in her campaign and communication strategies. Ocasio-Cortez demonstrated more than a new future for the Democratic Party. She also made a new future for politics seem possible.

ALEXANDRIA OCASIO-CORTEZ

Write your answers on a separate piece of paper.

1. Write a paragraph that summarizes the main ideas of the Green New Deal.

2. Are Ocasio-Cortez's ideas popular where you live? Why or why not?

3. Which organization first asked Ocasio-Cortez to run for Congress?

    A. Democratic Socialists of America
    B. Brand New Congress
    C. Democratic Party

4. Why do people consider Ocasio-Cortez to be progressive?

    A. Her ideas try to uphold traditional values.
    B. Her ideas try to make government less active in the economy.
    C. Her ideas try to bring change and social reform.

Answer key on page 48.

GLOSSARY

capitalism
An economic system in which people own property and work to make money.

constituents
People who live in a representative's district.

district
An area that votes to elect a representative.

global warming
An increase in the average global temperature, caused by pollutants that trap heat in the atmosphere.

greenhouse gas emissions
Gases that are released into the atmosphere by factories, cars, and many other sources, contributing to global warming.

immigration
The process of moving to a new country to live permanently.

primary
An election that decides a political party's nominee for a general election.

progressive
In favor of making changes or improvements away from traditional norms, especially relating to political or social issues.

public policy
Government rules that affect the entire population of a country.

socialist
Supporting a political system in which the government provides for basic needs, and where workers control the economy.

TO LEARN MORE

BOOKS

Harris, Duchess, with Laura K. Murray. *Class and Race*. Minneapolis: Abdo Publishing, 2019.

Lanser, Amanda. *Women in Politics and Government*. Minneapolis: Abdo Publishing, 2017.

McPherson, Stephanie Sammartino. *Political Parties: From Nominations to Victory Celebrations*. Minneapolis: Lerner Publications, 2016.

NOTE TO EDUCATORS

Visit **www.focusreaders.com** to find lesson plans, activities, links, and other resources related to this title.

INDEX

Answer Key: 1. Answers will vary; 2. Answers will vary; 3. B; 4. C